A Day in York

City Explorer

Read With You Center for Excellence
in STEAM Education

Published by Read With You Publishing
Designed by Read With You Center for Language Research and Development
Read With You and associated logos are trademarks and/or registered trademarks of Read With You L.L.C.
ISBN-13: 979-8-88618-195-1
First Edition April 2022
Printed in the United States of America.

Tim is a photojournalist. He takes exciting photos of places across the globe! But he needs someone to tell him what he's looking at. Today he's in an English city known for its historic buildings.

Jacob is a researcher who also explores the world, but from his home. He helps Tim understand the sights he sees. Jacob will guide Tim through this city that blends old and new.

Another fascinating city! Are you ready, Jacob? What should I know about Clifford's Tower?

The tower is all that's left of York Castle. It was a government building back in the thirteenth century. But you're in luck! It is newly renovated.

I have a great view of York. I bet guards used to watch out for enemies from here. How exactly was this tower used?

Well, Clifford's Tower was part of the wall that went all around York. The castle itself was used as a treasury, a court, and a jail.

It sounds like a busy place!
Is this the river that runs
through York on my map?

Yes! Rivers are excellent
places to build cities because
they provide water and
transportation. York was built
around the River Ouse.

These residents seemed to have lived well. I'm in the Fairfax House. Let me tell you, I wish I had bookshelves like these.

Me, too. The house is in Georgian style, which was fashionable in the 1700s. The house's owner was a viscount, a kind of English noble.

George as in the English kings? I see lots of symmetry in this style. I also feel like I'm peeking into someone's private life!

The Fairfax family was important in York. They hosted big parties and were close friends with noble families, so a lot of history happened here!

And now on to a different museum: The Merchant Adventurers' Hall. That's such an exciting name!

The Merchant Adventurers was really an economic, religious, and charitable organization. Check out the Great Hall and the Chapel to learn more.

The exhibits tell me that a religious group of merchants used this space to take care of the poor.

That's right! The hall was built in the mid-1300s and has been used ever since. But today it's mostly a museum.

I've worked up an appetite! I think I'll try some Yorkshire pudding. I hear it's a dish the locals eat.

It must be great, since Yorkshire pudding started there! Try it with gravy. Enjoy the bread-like taste!

Mm! You were right, pudding
and gravy is a delight.
Let's carry on! This must be
another part of York's wall.

Yes, it's the old city walls again.
They had four gates that you can
still view today. They were the
main entrances into
fortified York.

I see one of them now! It looks like it would be hard to sneak through. Why did York need so much protection?

The king often stayed in York Castle. See the holes in the rock? Guards could shoot arrows at enemies from there.

I want something more peaceful. This view will do! The trees and church make a nice sight.

You should stop inside the York Minster. The building's history goes back to the seventh century, and the architecture inside is stunning.

Wow, you're right! I always love stained glass windows. The colors and lighting are so delicate.

Some of the windows are almost a thousand years old. The church's caretakers are glazing them to preserve them for years to come.

I think of old buildings as simply existing. But you're right. If buildings aren't cared for, they'll fall apart like this one.

That's right. St. Mary's Abbey was a monastery. It was first built in 1088, but rediscovered in the 1800s. Now it's one of many ruins in York.

I love old places! But I'll round off my trip with an iconic English dish everyone still loves. It's time for fish and chips.

Yum! Don't forget to put vinegar and salt on them. Enjoy!

TO LET

I'm glad I could learn about
York's history today.
Thank you for your help!

You're welcome. It's amazing to see places that have lasted so long. Safe travels back home!

Learn

1. What old remains can you find around York?

2. Why was York so well protected?

3. What was the purpose of the Merchant Adventurers' Hall?

4. What do people typically eat with Yorkshire pudding?

Imagine

1. Which sites would you most like to visit in York? Why?

2. If you wanted to build a solid defense around your home, how would you do so?

3. Why do you think some buildings are kept up beautifully, like York Minster, and some are left in ruins, like St. Mary's Abbey?

4. Would you prefer to eat fish and chips or Yorkshire pudding? Why?

Act

Option 1

Research the city walls around York. What different groups built them? Why were they built? Write a paragraph about what you find.

Option 2

Design your own stained glass! Stained glass windows are typically made from pieces of colored glass that form a pattern. You can find examples online if you need inspiration. First, draw the pieces in your window. Then, fill in each section with a color.